smartypanthers
STUDIO

PUBLISHED BY SMARTY PANTHERS STUDIO 2024

Journey Through Riddle Castle: Alfie's Quest

An Adventure-Based Activity Book For the 11+ (Verbal Test Prep: Vocabulary Builder)

Targeted for Students Aged 8-9 / Early KS2

smartypanthers
STUDIO

Dear Parents and Guardians,

This short guide is intended to help your child get the most from this activity book.

We designed this book with a few aims. First, reinforce understanding and the correct spelling of words your child already knows, and second, introduce them to new words to help expand their vocabulary.

If your child doesn't know a word, get them to look in the dictionary to learn the correct meaning. It's also helpful if you can find an image that represents the word they are trying to learn, as a visual representation may help their understanding.

Some general tips. Encourage your child to take regular breaks. We've kept this book relatively short and bite-size. The goal here is more than expanding their vocabulary knowledge skills - it's about having fun while learning words and building confidence. Regular breaks from the questions will help with that.

The Smarty Panthers Studio Team

smartypanthers
STUDIO

Contents

The Whispering Entrance Hall......................Page 10

The Enchanted Library..................................Page 19

The Royal Banquet Hall...............................Page 28

The Hall of Mirrors.......................................Page 35

The Garden of Echoes..................................Page 43

The Wizard's Tower.......................................Page 52

The Riddle Dungeon......................................Page 58

The Treasure Chamber.................................Page 66

Answers Page..Page 77

Dear Adventurer

Get ready to join Alfie on an exciting journey through Riddle Castle. Together, you'll explore mysterious corridors, secret gardens, and hidden rooms. Each chapter brings a new challenge and a chance to discover the magic of words. Are you prepared to help Alfie unlock secrets and find hidden treasures? Let's start this amazing adventure in the world of words!

Instructions

Follow the map: It guides you room by room.

*

Complete challenges: Solve exciting puzzles to advance.

*

Collect rewards: Earn keys to unlock new areas.

*

Reach the Treasure Chamber for the ultimate word mastery challenge!

*

Ready to start? Turn the page and begin your adventure!

Adventurer Tips

Take your time: No need to rush! Enjoy each puzzle and learn at your own pace

*

Ask for help: If you're stuck, it's okay to seek help. Two heads are often better than one!

*

Enjoy the journey: Relish every puzzle, word, and secret you uncover.

*

Keep a notebook handy: down new words and ideas; they're treasures, too.

Adventurer Tips

Be curious: Remember: discovering new words is part of the adventure!

*

Celebrate your achievements: Each completed challenge marks your progress!

*

Use a dictionary if you get stuck on a word. A thesaurus is also super helpful!

Wizard's Tower
Riddle Dungeon
Garden of Echoes
Treasure Chamber
Hall of Mirrors
Royal Banquet Hall
Enchanted Library
Whispering Entrance Hall
CASTLE MAP

The Whispering Entrance Hall

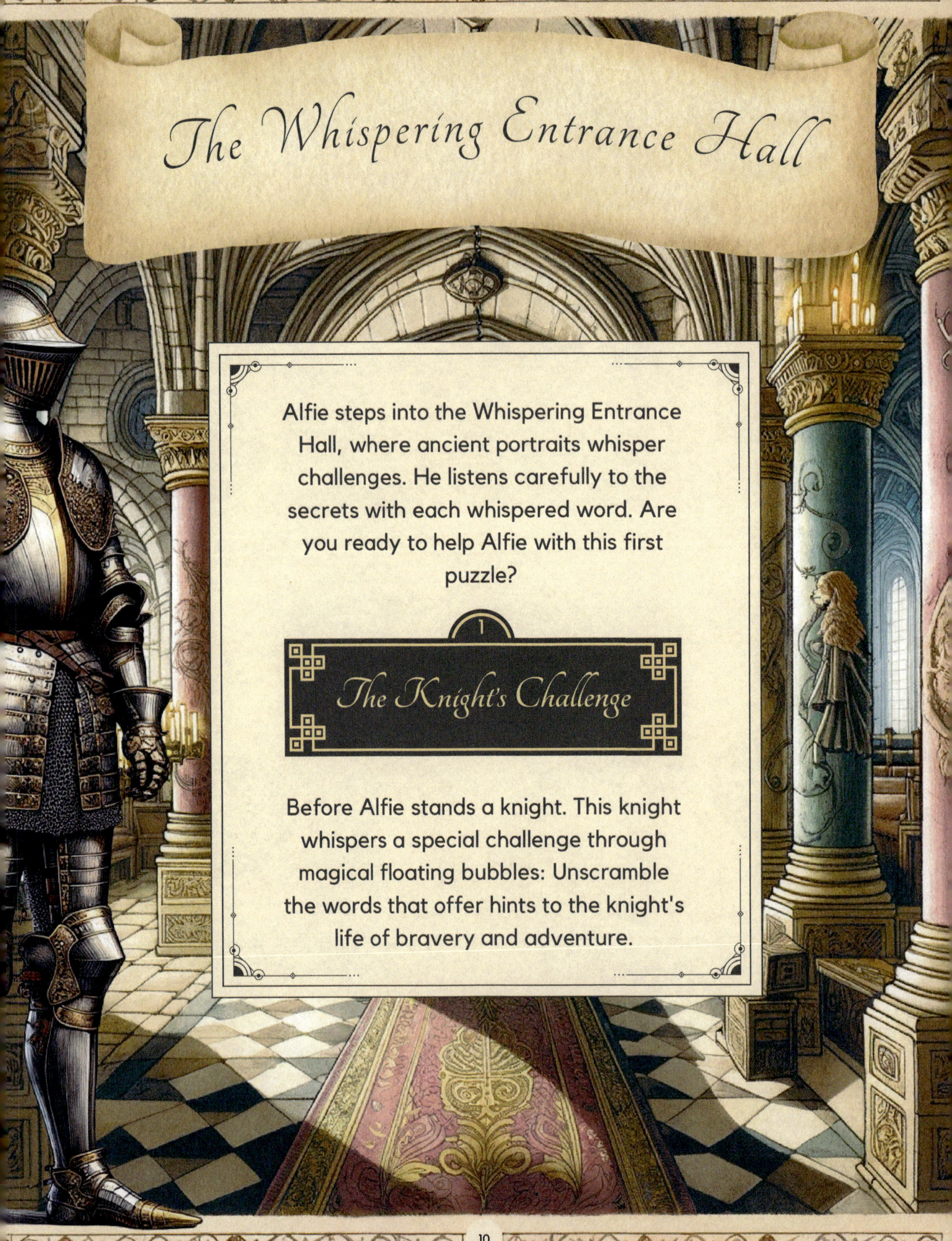

Alfie steps into the Whispering Entrance Hall, where ancient portraits whisper challenges. He listens carefully to the secrets with each whispered word. Are you ready to help Alfie with this first puzzle?

1 The Knight's Challenge

Before Alfie stands a knight. This knight whispers a special challenge through magical floating bubbles: Unscramble the words that offer hints to the knight's life of bravery and adventure.

The Whispering Entrance Hall

C E A
R U G
O

C _ _ R _ _ _

L E B
O N

_ _ B L _

T Q U
E S

Q _ _ S _

T A L I
V N A

V _ _ I _ _ _

V E
B R
A

_ R _ V _

The Whispering Entrance Hall

2

The Queen's Riddles

In the Whispering Entrance Hall, Alfie finds the portrait of Queen Eleanor with her Royal Scrolls. Each scroll contains a riddle that reveals the five qualities of a wise monarch: **Strong, Jovial, Graceful, Humble, Wise.** Let's help Alfie solve these riddles!

The Whispering Entrance Hall

With my knowledge, decisions are right;
in a queen's mind, I am the guiding light.

Not boasting, but always present; in a
queen's manner, I am pleasantly evident.

I don't make noise, but I'm lovely to see;
like a ballerina, I move smoothly and free.

In face of challenges, I stand tall,
showing power, not to fall.

In royal halls where laughter flows, I
make hearts lighter, as everyone knows.

The Whispering Entrance Hall

3

The Musician's Melody Match

As Alfie continues through the whispering hall, he encounters a musician with a puzzled look. He's forgotten the words to his songs and needs your help! Each tune has a missing rhyme. You'll find the words floating around the room, but only a sharp mind like yours can fill in the blanks. Can you help the musician find the missing rhymes and bring his music back to life?

The Whispering Entrance Hall

keen

With tricks up his sleeve in a mystical craze, the magician's acts never fail to ______

In the sky, shining with all its might, the moon at night is so very ______

amaze

jolly

The fox escapes the hunters' endeavor, with a cunning plan that's ever so ______

The eagle spots things rarely seen, with eyes so sharp, and a vision so ______

quick

clever

In the castle's halls, laughter and folly, the jester's jokes keep everyone ______

In the castle walls, with a clever trick, the knights train for battle, strong and ______

bright

The Whispering Entrance Hall

Alfie continues through the Whispering Entrance Hall, marvelling at its wonders. Can you match the majestic nouns to their descriptive adjectives?

4

The Majestic Matching Quest

Regal **Woven** **Sparkling**

Plush **Arched** **Smouldering**

______	Carpet	______	Tapestry
______	Throne	______	Chandelier
______	Window	______	Hearth

The Whispering Entrance Hall

Deep within the Whispering Hall, Alfie comes across a beautifully etched doorway, sealed with a magic spell. This challenge calls upon his knowledge of words and their hidden secrets to open the door.

5

The First Door Challenge

Find 5 words hidden in this word search door. (Hint: you've discovered these words on your journey already!). When you have found the five words, take one letter from each word using these rules. After you've found the 5 letters, rearrange it to make another word: your secret password to open the door.

RULE NUMBER ONE
The word begins with a letter from A to F in the alphabet

Find the third letter in that word

RULE NUMBER TWO
The word begins with a letter from G to I in the alphabet

Find the eighth letter in that word

RULE NUMBER THREE
The word begins with a letter from J to M in the alphabet

Find the fifth letter in that word

RULE NUMBER FOUR
The word begins with a letter from N to Z in the alphabet

Find the fourth letter in that word

(Hint: The Queen expects everyone in her castle to be _ _ _ _ _)

The Whispering Entrance Hall

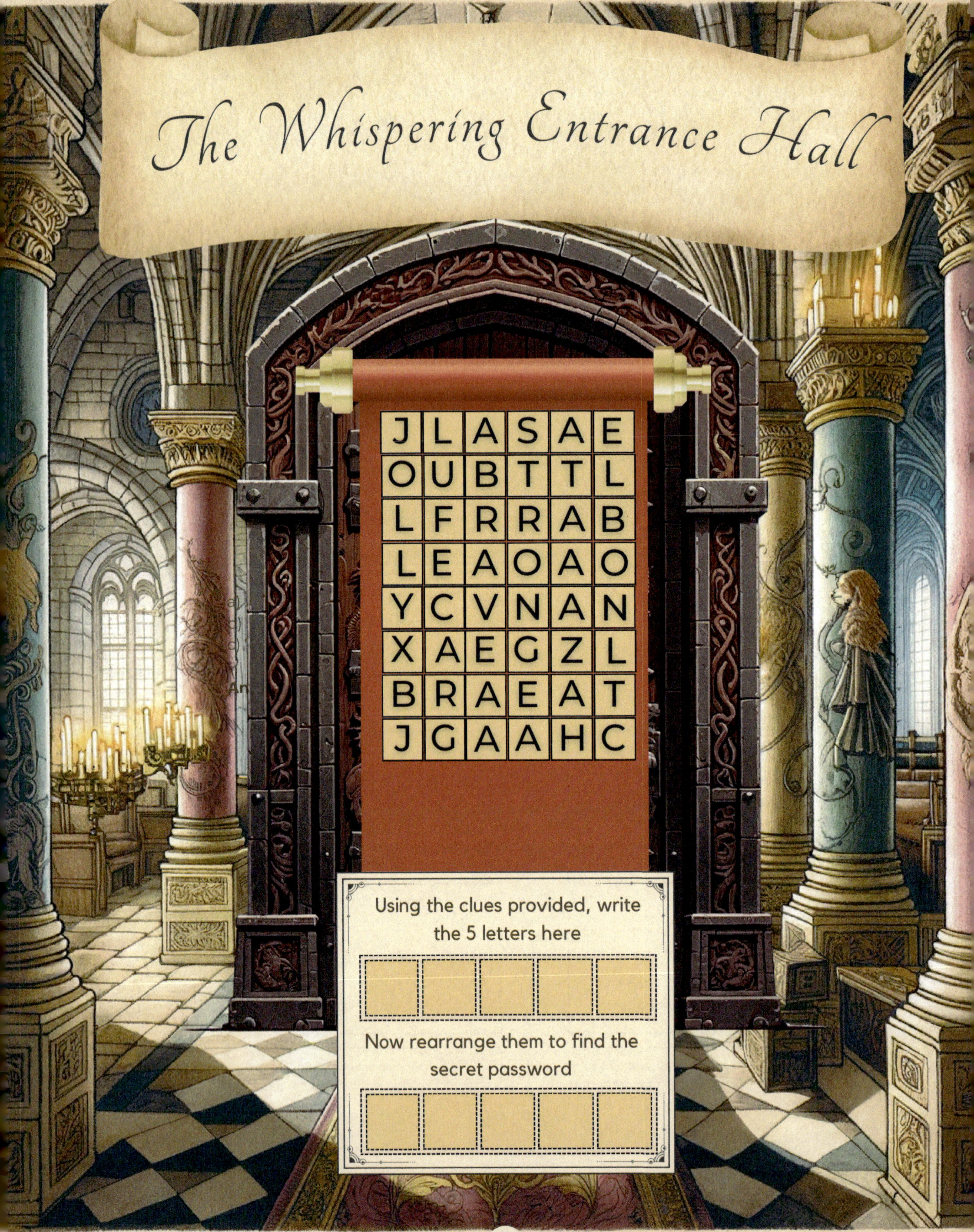

J	L	A	S	A	E
O	U	B	T	T	L
L	F	R	R	A	B
L	E	A	O	A	O
Y	C	V	N	A	N
X	A	E	G	Z	L
B	R	A	E	A	T
J	G	A	A	H	C

Using the clues provided, write the 5 letters here

Now rearrange them to find the secret password

The Enchanted Library

6

Elara the Owl's Mystical Word Web

Welcome to the Enchanted Library! Here, Alfie meets Elara, the wise owl librarian, who introduces him to the Mystical Word Web. Elara hands Alfie this magical web. Your task? Decide whether the words on the books relate to the first web - adventure, or the second web - happy.

The Enchanted Library

Joyful
Journey
Explore
Enthusiastic
Adventure
Grateful
Rescue
Cheerful
Discover
Gleeful
Happy
Voyage
Bonus activity:
Can you think of any other words to add to these word webs?

The Enchanted Library

7

The Hidden Portal: Connie's Adventure

In the Enchanted Library, Alfie finds an unfinished book. It's about a brave village girl called Connie. Connie finds a mysterious, ancient portal to another world. The story begins, but where it goes next is up to you. Around you, magical words float in the air, ready to be used in your tale. Help finish the story. Let your imagination guide you, and use as many floating words as possible!

The Enchanted Library

dazzle mysterious

As Connie gently pushed the old door, it creaked open, revealing a world unlike any she had seen before. In this strange land....

flutter

blossom

curious

magical

treasure playful

The Enchanted Library

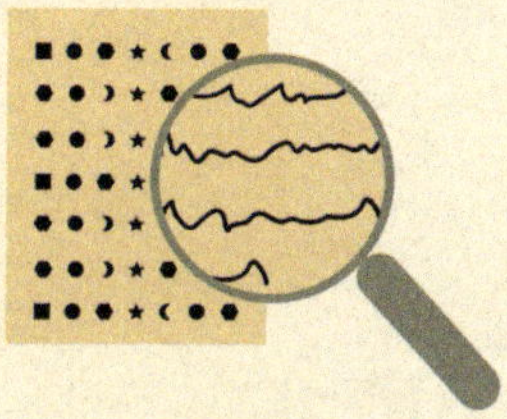

8

The Code Breaker

Alfie discovers a mysterious book in the library with a magical code. It's hiding a message. Can you decode the book and discover the hidden message? To crack the code, look at the following symbols and their corresponding letters.

The Enchanted Library

A	○	B	△	O	☾	P	✪
C	□	D	★	Q	⬢	R	✻
E	✦	F	♦	S	⊕	T	✚
G	⬟	H	✜	U	♣	V	⊠
I	♦	J	%	W	✳	X	×
K	✤	L	◇	Y	!	Z	☺
M	⊠	N	☼				

☾☼◇! ○ ★○✻♦☼⬟ ○★⊠✦☼✚♣✻✦✻

□○☼ ♣☼□☾⊠✦✻ ✚✜✦ ♣☼♦⬢♣✦

✤☼☾✳◇✦★⬟✦ ✜♦★★✦☼ ♦☼ ✚✜✦

□○⊕✚◇✦ ✳○◇◇⊕

_ _ _ _   _   _ _ _ _ _ _   _ _ _ _ _ _ _ _ _ _

_ _ _   _ _ _ _ _ _ _   _ _ _   _ _ _ _ _ _

_ _ _ _ _ _ _ _ _   _ _ _ _ _ _   _ _

_ _ _   _ _ _ _ _ _   _ _ _ _ _

The Enchanted Library

9

The Unfinished Story

Alfie discovers an unfinished story left on the table in the middle of the enchanted library. The author has left clues to the missing words - they are all book titles from the library! Use the missing words to complete the tale.

In the [ ] kingdom of Fireola, a brave knight named Sir Marcus embarked on a quest to find the [ ] dragon that had been [ ] the villagers. Armed with his [ ] sword and [ ] shield, he trekked through the [ ] forest. After days of searching, he finally found the dragon's [ ] in a mountain cave. To his surprise, the dragon was not fierce but rather [ ]. They talked for hours and realised that a misunderstanding had caused the [ ] between the dragon and the village. Sir Marcus returned to the village, not with a story of battle, but with a [ ] of friendship and peace.

- dense
- sharp
- tale
- lair
- peaceful
- conflict
- friendly
- protective
- fearsome
- frightening

The Enchanted Library

Behind a shelf of books in the library, you come across another secret doorway sealed with a magic spell. This challenge calls upon the words you've found in the enchanted library.

10

The Second Door Challenge

Find 5 words hidden in this word search door. (Hint: you've discovered these words in the library already!). When you have found the five words, take one letter from each word using these rules. After you've found the 5 letters, rearrange it to make another word: your secret password to open the door.

RULE NUMBER ONE
The word begins with a letter from A to G in the alphabet

Find the fourth letter in that word

RULE NUMBER TWO
The word begins with a letter from H to L in the alphabet

Find the first letter in that word

RULE NUMBER THREE
The word begins with a letter from M to Q in the alphabet

Find the third letter in that word

RULE NUMBER FOUR
The word begins with a letter from R to Z in the alphabet

Find the fifth letter in that word

(Hint: When the queen tells a joke, she expects everyone to _ _ _ _ _)

The Enchanted Library

N	B	A	E	A	R
L	D	L	R	U	E
A	W	U	O	A	S
C	L	F	L	S	C
I	C	Y	P	A	U
G	A	A	X	Q	E
A	F	L	E	A	A
M	Y	P	P	A	H

Using the clues provided, write the 5 letters here

Now rearrange them to find the secret password

The Royal Banquet Hall

11

The Monarch's Menu Challenge

Welcome to The Monarch's Menu Challenge! Your task is to help Alfie create a majestic menu fit for royalty. The chef has jotted down some word ideas - choose the best ones to name and describe each dish, making your menu as splendid as the banquet itself. After that, have some fun colouring in the pictures of the dishes to make the menu look appetising.

The Royal Banquet Hall

brilliant

sumptuous

hearty

succulent

rustic

fragrant

sizzling

aromatic

fantastic

wholesome

surprise

warm

MENU

____________ Roast Chicken

____________ Garden Salad

____________ Spring Vegetable Soup

____________ Treacle Pudding

____________ Hunter's Pie

____________ Winter Stew

____________ Apple Tart

The Royal Banquet Hall

The Royal Chef has created a wonderful feast for the Queen and her subjects. But the mischievous Pixie Pippin has muddled up the guests' dishes! Fortunately, the Royal Assistant has left some clues on the table. Can you draw lines to join up the words on the goblets to the correct platter and help the chef prepare the feast?

12

Pixie Pippin's Menu Muddle

Plentiful; used to describe a banquet table filled with lots of different foods

To provide banquet guests with the food necessary for growth and health

Nourish

Great pleasure; the feeling guests have when enjoying delicious banquet dishes

Enormous

Opulent

Delight

Very large; used to describe the huge size of a banquet feast

Quirky

Odd in a fun and interesting way, like an unusual banquet dish

A very fancy banquet filled with expensive things

Skilful

Abundant

Mischief

Describes the talent of chefs in preparing and impressively presenting banquet meals

Naughty or playful behaviour at a banquet, causing a little trouble

The Royal Banquet Hall

13

The Banquet Hall's Word Feast

In the bustling kitchen of the Royal Banquet Hall, Alfie Meets Chef Gaston. He is busy preparing the menu for a magnificent feast. However, in the excitement, he's mixed up some of the words used to describe the delicious dishes! Help Alfie get the menu ready for the feast. Find the two words in each description that mean the same thing and circle them.

The Royal Banquet Hall

The Appetiser

Commence Begin Delicious Eating

Soup Course

Unseen Hidden Leap Actual

The Main Dish

Noble Common Royal Engage

Dessert

Make-believe Gallop Imaginary Observe

Drinks

Brave Recline Decline Fearless

The Royal Banquet Hall

At the end of the banquet hall, you come across another doorway sealed with a magic spell. This challenge calls upon the words you've found in the enchanted library.

14

The Third Door Challenge

Find 5 words hidden in this word search door. (Hint: you've discovered these words in the hall already!). When you have found the five words, take one letter from each word using these rules. After you've found the 5 letters, rearrange it to make another word: your secret password to open the door.

RULE NUMBER ONE
The word begins with a letter from A to H in the alphabet

Find the sixth letter in that word

RULE NUMBER TWO
The word begins with a letter from I to M in the alphabet

Find the fourth letter in that word

RULE NUMBER THREE
The word begins with a letter from N to O in the alphabet

Find the third letter in that word

RULE NUMBER FOUR
The word begins with a letter from P to Z in the alphabet

Find the fifth letter in that word

Hint: The Queen feels very _ _ _ _ to live in such a grand and beautiful castle.

The Royal Banquet Hall

M	R	T	L	O	G
I	A	H	E	P	N
S	D	E	Y	U	I
C	P	A	K	L	L
H	I	R	R	E	Z
I	A	T	I	N	Z
E	C	Y	U	T	I
F	F	U	Q	Q	S

Using the clues provided, write the 5 letters here

Now rearrange them to find the secret password

The Hall of Mirrors

Welcome to the mesmerizing Hall of Mirrors! This magical room in the castle is filled with countless mirrors of all shapes and sizes, each reflecting images and words in intriguing ways.

15

The Reflective Words

The mirrors don't just reflect images; they also hold hidden words, twisted and turned in their reflections.
Help Alfie identify each word by reading its mirror reflection and then write it correctly.

The Hall of Mirrors

Fantastic
Yearn
Imitate
Clumsy
Surprise
Invisible
Harmony
Gentle

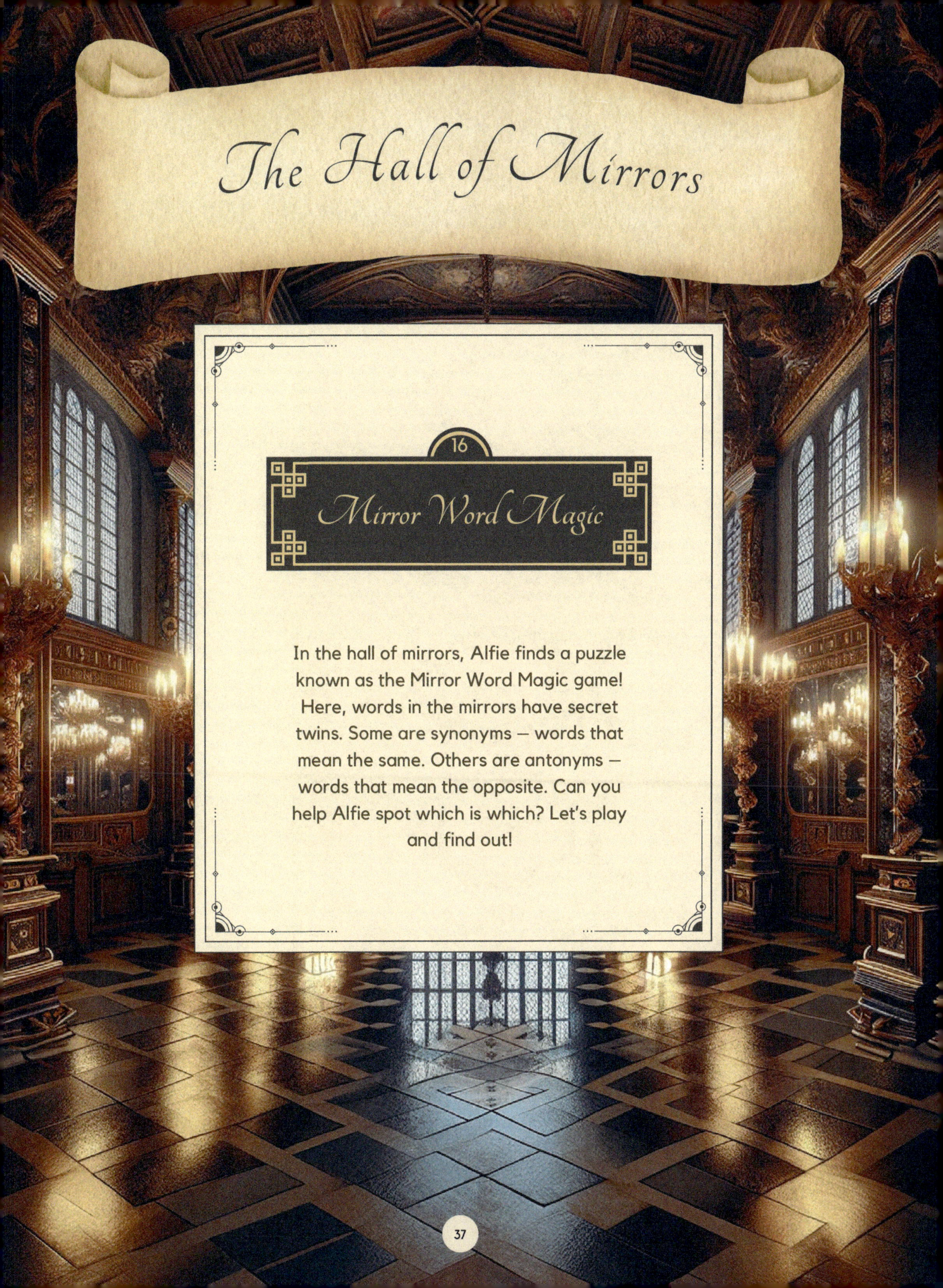

The Hall of Mirrors

16

Mirror Word Magic

In the hall of mirrors, Alfie finds a puzzle known as the Mirror Word Magic game! Here, words in the mirrors have secret twins. Some are synonyms – words that mean the same. Others are antonyms – words that mean the opposite. Can you help Alfie spot which is which? Let's play and find out!

The Hall of Mirrors

Melancholy	Joyful	☐ the same ☐ opposites
Amiable	Friendly	☐ the same ☐ opposites
Courageous	Fearless	☐ the same ☐ opposites
Generous	Mean	☐ the same ☐ opposites
Tranquil	Serene	☐ the same ☐ opposites
Curious	Unconcerned	☐ the same ☐ opposites

The Hall of Mirrors

17

The Hall of Mirrors Word Wonders

The Hall of Mirrors is filled with words written in stone and their meanings are reflected on mirrors. Alfie needs your help to match the clues to the correct words. By solving them, you'll help Alfie navigate through the hall and uncover the magic of language. Draw a line from each clue to the word it describes

The Hall of Mirrors

Mischievous

To make room or adjust to fit

A desire to learn or know about anything

Curiosity

Sincere

Happening or occurring often

Frequent

Playfully naughty or troublesome

Opportunity

A chance for progress or advancement

Accommodate

Free from pretence or deceit; genuine

The Hall of Mirrors

18

The Fourth Door Challenge

In the Hall of Mirrors, a ghostly figure, Lady Luminara, guards the key to the Garden of Echoes. To pass through the locked door, Alfie must provide the secret word! Help Alfie find his way through Lady Luminara's word maze. Each correct word brings you closer to the secret word. Choose wisely and unlock your path to the enchanted Garden of Echoes!

The Hall of Mirrors

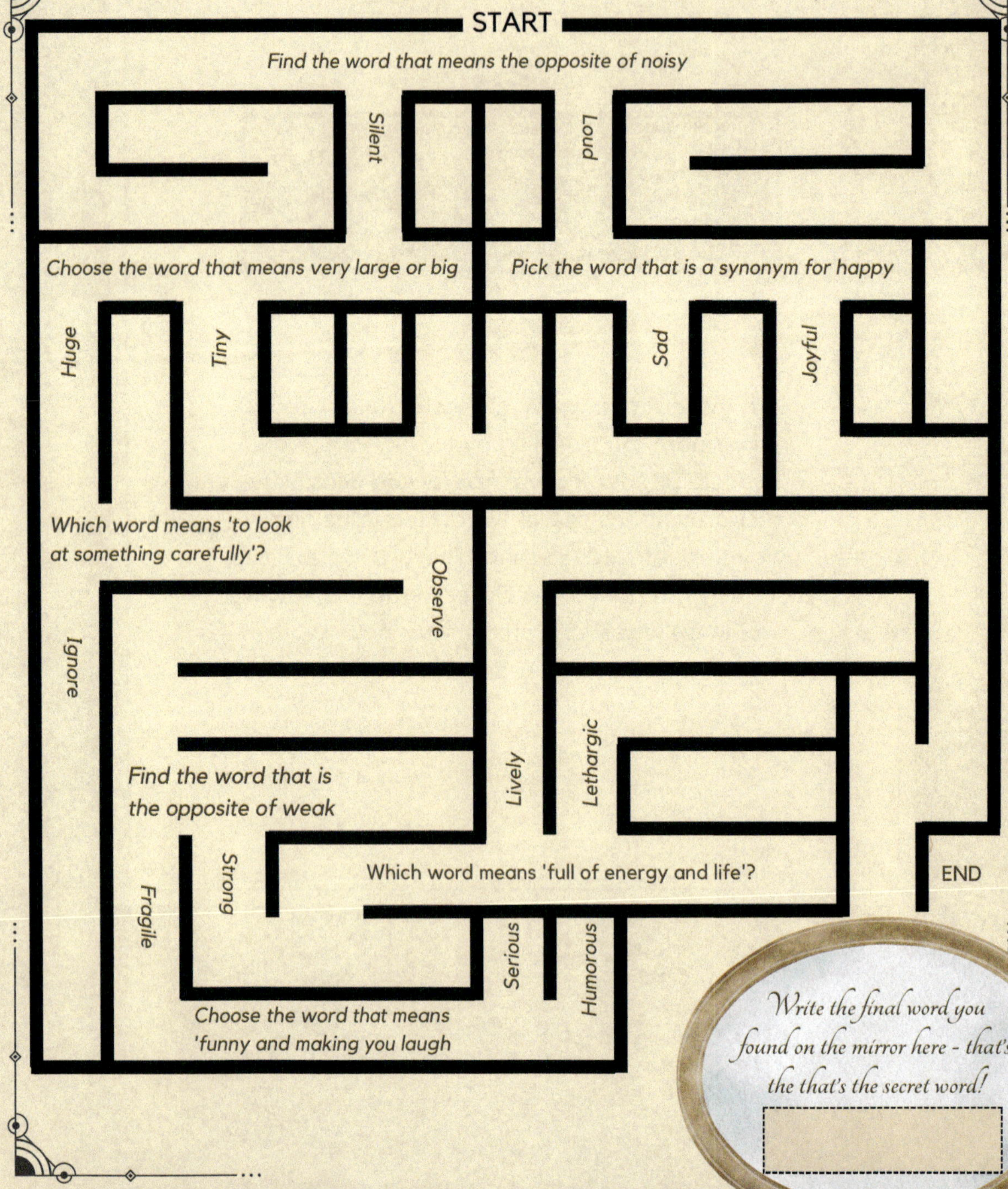
START
Find the word that means the opposite of noisy
Silent
Loud
Choose the word that means very large or big
Pick the word that is a synonym for happy
Huge
Tiny
Sad
Joyful
Which word means 'to look at something carefully'?
Observe
Ignore
Lethargic
Lively
Find the word that is the opposite of weak
Strong
Fragile
Which word means 'full of energy and life'?
END
Serious
Humorous
Choose the word that means 'funny and making you laugh

Write the final word you found on the mirror here - that's the that's the secret word!

The Garden of Echoes

As Alfie steps into the Garden of Echoes, he's greeted by a symphony of whispers and rustling leaves. This enchanted space, alive with ancient magic, holds secrets waiting to be discovered. Here, every echo tells a tale, and every shadow dances with the past. Alfie's curiosity is ignited, eager to explore its mysteries.

19

The Whispering Willow's Word Branches

In the heart of the Garden of Echoes, Whispering Willow, a wise and ancient talking tree, invites Alfie to a unique word challenge. His branches are adorned with word stems, each needing the right prefix or suffix to grow into a full word. Help Alfie find six new words growing in the tree and write them on the signposts below.

The Garden of Echoes

re-
over-
un-
-ness
-ly
-ful
happy
play
power
grow
kind
friend

The Garden of Echoes

20

The Echoes of Ancient Stories

The Garden of Echoes is not only a place of beauty but also of hidden stories. Each flower and leaf carries parts of a tale waiting to be woven together. Choose your favourite prompt from one of the four suggested on the leaves, and try to use as many words from the flowers as you can to write a short story. Let your imagination bloom!

The Garden of Echoes

Write the start of a story about a flower in the garden with a secret

Create a paragraph about a mysterious guest visiting the garden at night

Twinkle

Whisper

Blossom

Flutter

Describe how the garden looks in summer

Lush

Radiant

Write about the plants and flowers talking to each other

The Garden of Echoes

21

The Raindrop Misspell Mystery

The garden's whispers carry tales of magic and mystery, but the rain has muddled the story's words. Your mission is to help Alfie by spotting the rain-damaged words (misspelled words) in Elara's adventure and correcting them. Circle the incorrect letters, and write the correct versions below.

The Garden of Echoes

One day, Elara the pixie found a scrol in the Garden of Echos, revealing the Enchanted Tree's seecret. A gobblin, eagar for its majic, raced Elara to the tree. Through enchanted thickets and with the help of garden creatures, Elara outwitted the gobblin. As they reached the tree, her cleverness trapped him in a maze. Touching the tree, she released its majic, reviving the garden. Elara's bravery became legendary, a testament to courage and wit.

The Garden of Echoes

22

The Fifth Door Challenge

Beyond the Garden of Echoes lies a locked door leading to the Wizard's Tower. To unlock it, Alfie must cast a magic spell. Help Alfie by creating three compound words that fit perfectly into the gaps to complete the spell.

The Garden of Echoes

Thunder
Rain
Sun
Storm
Moon
Bell
Drop
Shine
Light

The Garden of Echoes

At night, the ________ rages overhead. A single ________ falls and glistens in the ________

The Wizard's Tower

Ascending the spiral staircase, Alfie enters the Wizard's Tower, a realm where magic breathes and spells weave the air. Surrounded by books and potions, he senses the power of ancient wisdom. This is where his magical journey takes flight.

23

Wizard Ivor's Enchanted Brew Formula

As Alfie steps into Wizard Ivor's tower, he's surrounded by mysterious potions and spellbooks. His task: help Ivor concoct a famous potion, but with a twist – every ingredient must be given a magical name. Can you help Alfie complete this enchanting recipe? Combine together words floating out of the books and be as inventive as you like to create the potion names.

The Wizard's Tower

fire sun night

cloud wind frost

star light moon

rain sea snow

wood water stone

flower glass heart

The Wizard's Tower

24

Wizard Ivor's Cauldron Conundrums

In Wizard Ivor's tower, Alfie discovers a mystical cauldron. To cast enchanting spells, he must select the perfect words! Help Alfie complete each spell with the right word. Stir your choice into the cauldron and watch the enchantment unfold!

The Wizard's Tower

To conjure this spell with magic and ease,
add in a touch of the ________ breeze

a) turret ☐
b) whispering ☐
c) potion ☐
d) quest ☐

To walk through walls, invisible and free,
stir in a drop of _______ sea

a) emerald ☐
b) sorcerer ☐
c) jester ☐
d) fable ☐

For a powerful potion that will make you fly,
add a fallen feather from a _______ sky

a) oracle ☐
b) dragon ☐
c) guitar ☐
d) stormy ☐

To speak as one with the flowers and trees,
add in a dash of these ________leaves

a) stone ☐
b) maple ☐
c) painting ☐
d) musician ☐

For a superpower that lets you talk with birds,
mix in a cup of some ________ words

a) magical ☐
b) frog ☐
c) window ☐
d) oak ☐

For dreams of future, near and far,
sprinkle in a dash of _______ star

a) chestnut ☐
b) twinkling ☐
c) discover ☐
d) happily ☐

The Wizard's Tower

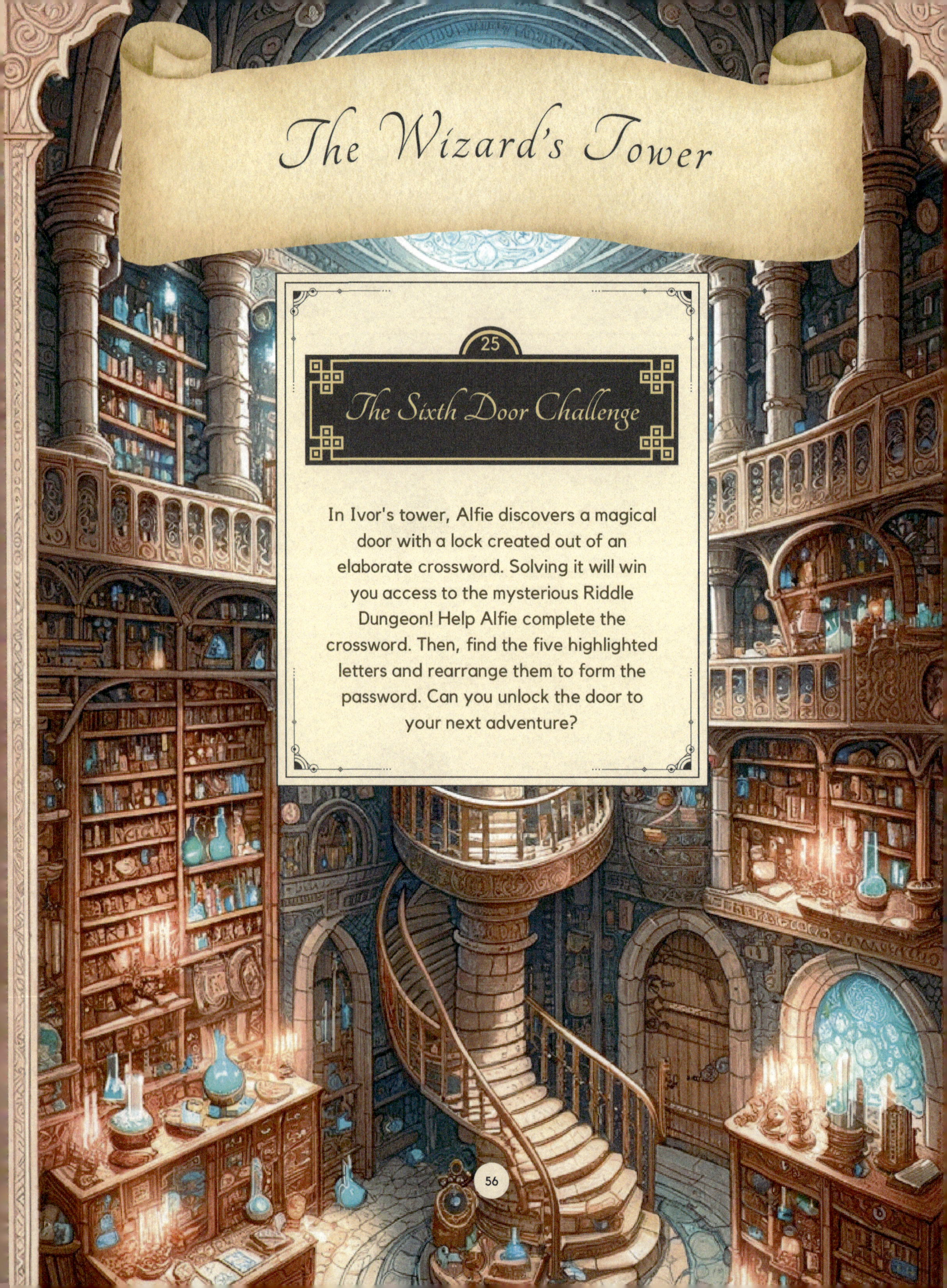

25

The Sixth Door Challenge

In Ivor's tower, Alfie discovers a magical door with a lock created out of an elaborate crossword. Solving it will win you access to the mysterious Riddle Dungeon! Help Alfie complete the crossword. Then, find the five highlighted letters and rearrange them to form the password. Can you unlock the door to your next adventure?

The Wizard's Tower

1
2
3
4
5

Clues

1 down: Find a synonym for "difficult" that starts with an 'H'
3 across: Find the opposite of "ancient."
4 down: Name a feathered creature that is known for its wisdom and often depicted in wizard stories
2 across: Find a word that means both a part of a tree and something a dog might do
5 Across: Find a word that describes a large stone building, often home to royalty, fortified against attack with thick walls and battlements.

The Secret Password Is: ☐☐☐☐☐

(Clue: A weapon with a long metal blade. Often associated with knights and battles in medieval times)

The Riddle Dungeon

Beneath the castle lies the Riddle Dungeon, a labyrinth of mysteries and conundrums. Here, Alfie faces puzzles that challenge the mind and spirit. Each solved riddle brings him closer to unlocking its secret.

26

Wisteria's Enchanted Enigmas

Alfie encounters the mysterious Witch Wisteria. She greets him with a smile, her eyes sparkling with ancient knowledge. She presents him with enchanting riddles as gateways to hidden secrets. Help Alfie solve Wisteria's riddles by deciphering the clues.

The Riddle Dungeon

I'm a word that means to 'reveal' something hidden. I have 7 letters and start with 'U'. What word am I?

U _ C _ V _ _

I mean the same as 'brave', have 7 letters, and start with 'C'. Someone who is not afraid to face danger has lots of this. What word am I?

C _ U _ _ G _

I'm the opposite of 'modern', have 7 letters, and start with 'A'. I'm used to describe something very old, especially something valuable from the past. What word am I?

A _ T _ Q _ _

I'm the opposite of 'enemy', have 6 letters, and start with 'F'. I'm someone you trust and enjoy spending time with. What word am I?

F R _ _ N _

I'm the opposite of 'articulate', have 6 letters, and start with 'M'. I'm used to describe speaking in a low, unclear voice. What word am I?

M _ M _ L _

The Riddle Dungeon

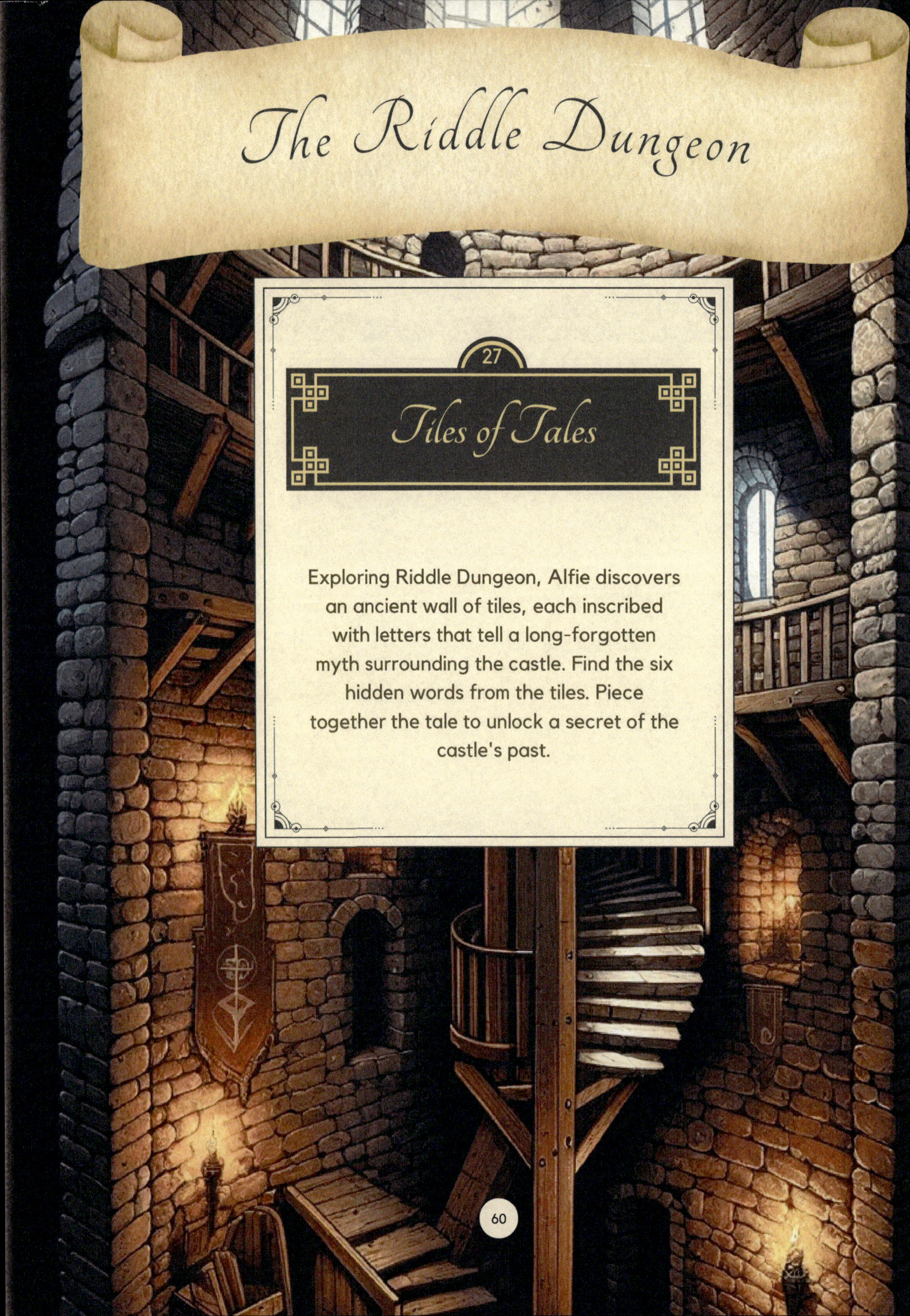

27

Tiles of Tales

Exploring Riddle Dungeon, Alfie discovers an ancient wall of tiles, each inscribed with letters that tell a long-forgotten myth surrounding the castle. Find the six hidden words from the tiles. Piece together the tale to unlock a secret of the castle's past.

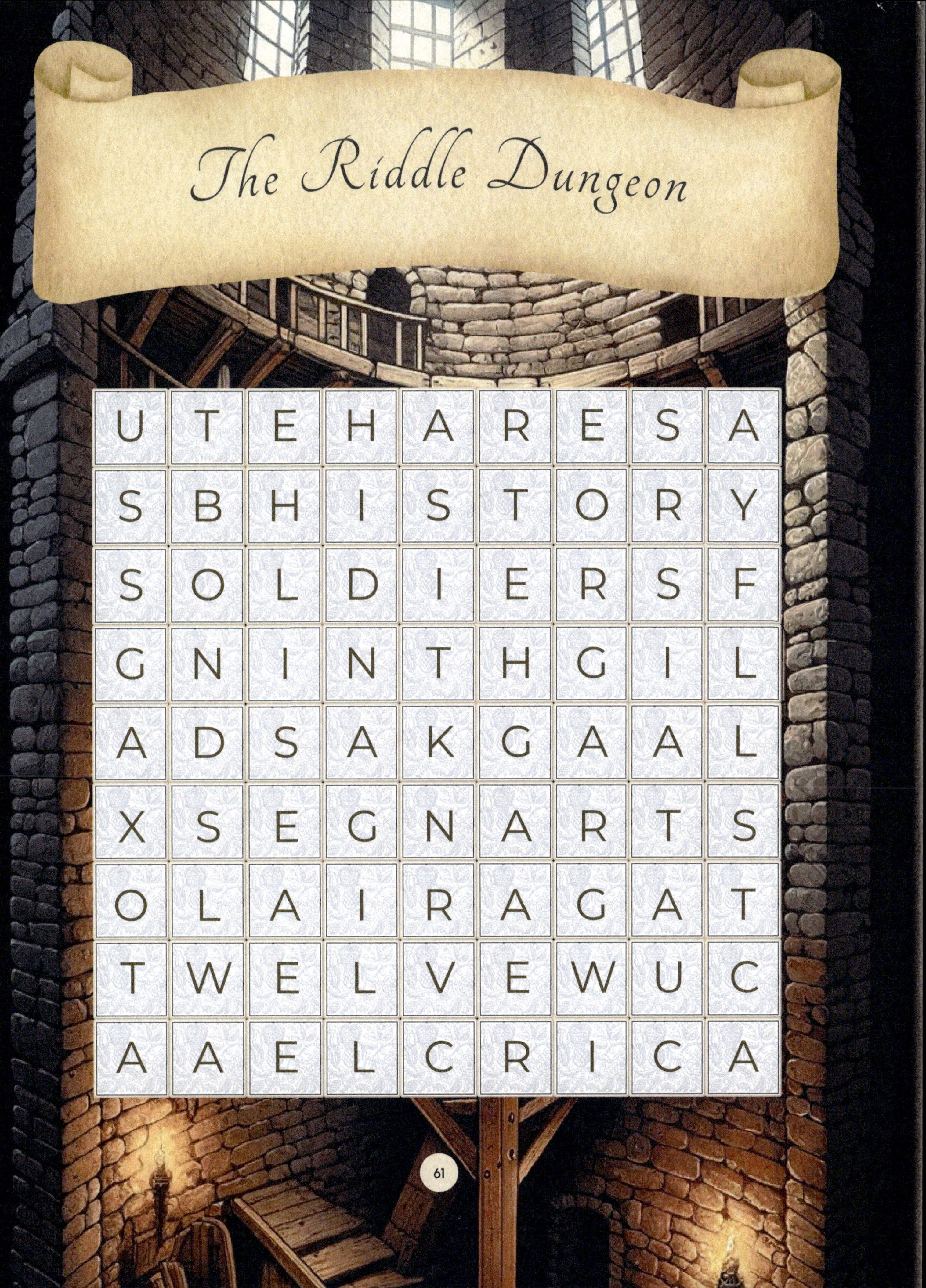

The Riddle Dungeon

U	T	E	H	A	R	E	S	A
S	B	H	I	S	T	O	R	Y
S	O	L	D	I	E	R	S	F
G	N	I	N	T	H	G	I	L
A	D	S	A	K	G	A	A	L
X	S	E	G	N	A	R	T	S
O	L	A	I	R	A	G	A	T
T	W	E	L	V	E	W	U	C
A	A	E	L	C	R	I	C	A

The Riddle Dungeon

In long-forgotten
h_s____, a st_____
tale is told of _w__v_
brave _ol__e__, stood
in a _i_c__, who
vanished in a flash of
_i___n_n_.

28

The Seventh Door Challenge

In the dimly lit corridor, Alfie finds a path of glowing stepping stones leading to a gilded door adorned with intricate runes. This majestic portal guards the secrets of the castle's heart. Help Alfie navigate the pathway by stepping on stones that form the correct sentence. Each correct word brings the luminous door closer to unlocking. Avoid the misleading trap words that threaten to lead Alfie astray in this labyrinth.

The Riddle Dungeon

The

sense

dragon

key

tower

beneath

is

the

jewel

hidden

ghost

ancient

stone

The Riddle Dungeon

The Treasure Chamber

Behind the golden door lies a treasure-filled chamber. The bedroom is surrounded by gold and royal treasures. Alfie is almost at the end of his adventure, excited to uncover the castle's mysteries he's about to fully unveil.

29

The Chamber's Misplaced Mysteries

In the Treasure Chamber, Alfie encounters inscriptions shimmering in gold, each narrating a tale that has been turned into a secret. Help Alfie to decipher these tales. You'll need to spot one misleading word in each set. Then, rearrange the remaining words to unveil the chamber's secrets.

The Treasure Chamber

the had castle a round
tree turret

knights brave the apple
defended kingdom from
invaders

forest the full
mysterious was magic
of clock

wizard the kingdom
spells the protect
dolphin used to

hosted the castle a king
hall in feast mirror the

the castle knight found
under treasure the toaster

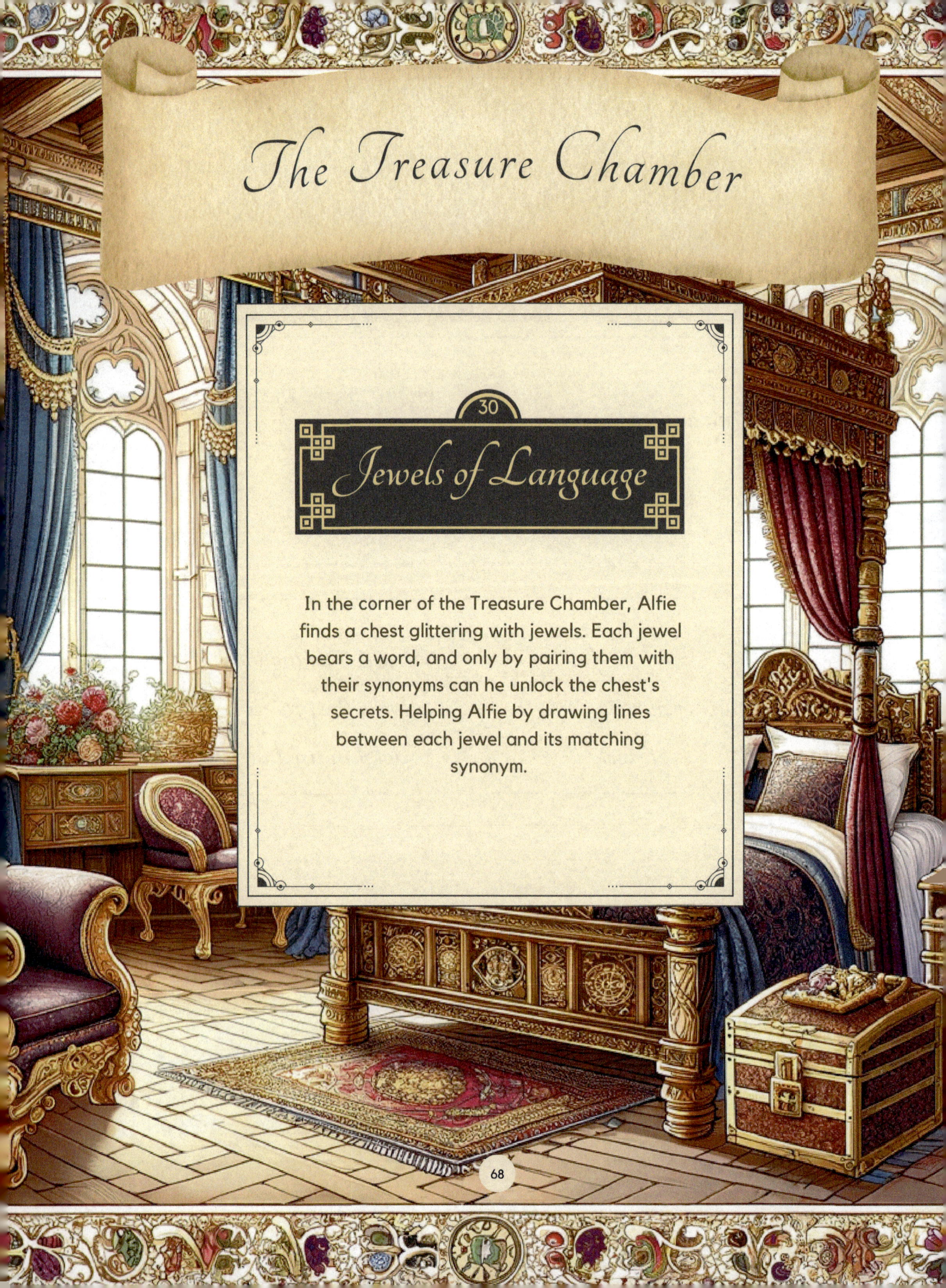

The Treasure Chamber

30

Jewels of Language

In the corner of the Treasure Chamber, Alfie finds a chest glittering with jewels. Each jewel bears a word, and only by pairing them with their synonyms can he unlock the chest's secrets. Helping Alfie by drawing lines between each jewel and its matching synonym.

The Treasure Chamber

weak
play
odd
blunder
feeble
smell
frolic
tall
ponder
odour
destiny
mistake
fate
think
lofty
peculiar

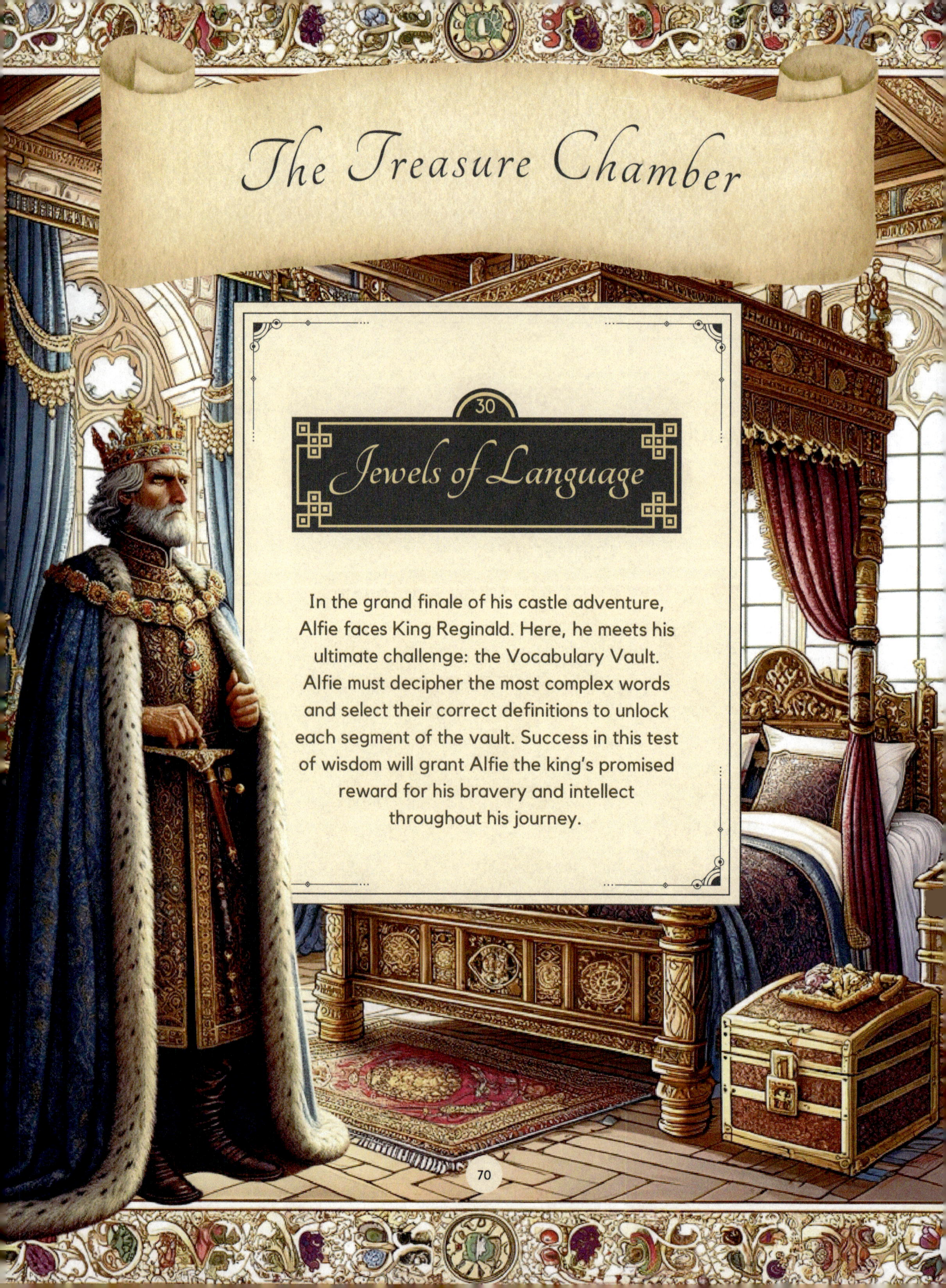

The Treasure Chamber

30

Jewels of Language

In the grand finale of his castle adventure, Alfie faces King Reginald. Here, he meets his ultimate challenge: the Vocabulary Vault. Alfie must decipher the most complex words and select their correct definitions to unlock each segment of the vault. Success in this test of wisdom will grant Alfie the king's promised reward for his bravery and intellect throughout his journey.

The Treasure Chamber

integrity	companion
majestic	formidable
protagonist	oath
endeavour	lavish
illuminate	exquisite

Making things bright or easy to understand, like lighting up a dark room or figuring out something hard.

Something really regal and grand, like this big, amazing castle.

Very beautiful and special, like the wonderful treasures Alfie found.

Very fancy and rich, like a big feast in the castle.

Something very strong and impressive, like a big, brave dragon.

Always telling the truth and being good, like a true and honest knight.

A friend who joins you on adventures, just like the friends Alfie made in the castle.

The main person in a story, like Alfie in his castle adventure.

Trying very hard to do something, like Alfie working hard to solve puzzles.

A very important promise, like the ones knights make to be brave.

You've Done It!

In the grand hall, King Reginald's voice echoes,

"Alfie, your quest has led to a revelation of our kingdom's oldest legend. On their ancient quest, the twelve brave soldiers discovered jewels of immense power hidden by the wizards' spells. These gems, locked away for centuries, were safeguarded beneath the stone you cleverly uncovered."

With a proud smile, the King presents Alfie with one of the luminous jewels.

"This is not just a reward but a key to untold adventures. Its magic, cast by our most esteemed wizards, grants you the ability to travel in time. Explore mysterious medieval castles and uncover stories lost to time."

Alfie, holding the magical jewel, felt the weight of history in his palm, excited for the doors it would open to the past.

Congratulations!

Well done for reaching the end of the castle. You've discovered so many words in this adventure. Why not use some of those to create your own story about what Alfie does next on his adventures? We've added an empty page if you want to do this. Here's a reminder of all the words you've learned throughout the book.

Abundant
Accommodate
Adventure
Adventurer
Amaze
Amiable
Ancient
Antique
Arched
Aromatic
Bark
Begin
Beneath
Blossom
Blunder
Brave
Bright
Brilliant
Carpet
Castle
Chandelier
Cheerful
Circle
Clever
Clumsy
Companion
Conflict
Courage
Courageous
Curiosity
Curious
Daring
Dazzle
Defended
Delight
Destiny
Discover
Eager
Echoes
Emerald
Endeavour
Enormous
Enthusiastic
Explore
Exquisite
Fantastic
Fate
Fearless
Fearsome
Feast
Feeble
Flutter
Forest
Formidable
Fragrant
Frequent
Friend
Friendly
Frightening
Frolic
Generous
Gentle
Gleeful
Goblin
Graceful
Grateful
Happily
Happiness
Happy
Hard
Harmony
Hearth
Hearty
Hidden
History
Hosted
Huge
Humble
Illuminate
Imaginary
Imitate
Integrity
Invaders
Invisible
Jolly
Journey
Jovial
Joyful

Congratulations!

Keen
Kindly
Kindness
Knowledge
Lair
Laugh
Lavish
Lightning
Lively
Lofty
Loyal
Lucky
Lush
Magic
Magical
Majestic
Maple
Mean
Melancholy
Mischief
Mischievous
Mistake
Modern
Moonlight
Mumble
Mysterious
Noble
Nourish
Oath
Observe
Odd
Odour
Opportunity
Opulent
Overgrow
Overplay
Overpower
Peaceful
Peculiar
Playful
Plush
Ponder
Powerful
Protagonist
Protect
Protective
Quest
Quick
Quirky
Radiant
Raindrop
Regal
Regrow
Replay
Rescue
Royal
Rustic
Scroll
Secret
Serene
Sharp
Silent
Sincere
Sizzling
Skilful
Smell
Smouldering
Soldiers
Sparkling
Spells
Stormy
Strange
Strong
Succulent
Sumptuous
Surprise
Sword
Tale
Tall
Tapestry
Think
Throne
Thunderstorm
Tranquil
Treasure
Turret
Twelve
Twinkle
Twinkling
Unconcerned
Uncover
Unhappy
Unique
Unkind
Unseen
Valiant
Voyage
Warm
Weak
Whisper
Whispering
Wholesome
Window
Wise
Wizard
Woven
Yearn

Your Story

Attention Parents

Dear Parent or Guardian,

Bravo! Your bright, determined child has triumphantly completed Alfie's quest, uncovering the secret password. We're thrilled to celebrate this milestone with you! You can get a special certificate and reward from us to recognise their efforts. To order it, please head to this link and add the secret password and your contact details (only parents can do this!).

https://smartypanthers.com/rewards/

We are a small, family-run UK start-up with a passion for supporting education. We are on an ambitious mission to turn learning into something more engaging, fun and accessible to every child. And we are grateful for your support.

But we need a small favour. If you have two minutes, we would be eternally grateful if you would leave a review on Amazon. Let us know your thoughts on the book so that other families can discover the adventures we create.

You can review the book by searching for the title "Alfie's Quest 11+ Workbook) and click on the **add review** option.

Thank you for joining us on this exciting educational journey. Your child's success and enthusiasm inspire us to create more enriching adventures!

Warmly,

The Smarty Panthers Studio Team

Answers Page

1: The Knight's Challenge

Courage
Noble
Quest
Valiant
Brave

2: The Queen's Riddles

Wise
Humble
Graceful
Strong
Jovial

3. The Musician's Melody Match

Amaze
Bright
Clever
Keen
Jolly
Quick

4. The Majestic Matching Quest

Woven Tapestry
Sparkling Chandelier
Smouldering Hearth
Regal Throne
Plush Carpet
Arched Window

5. The First Door Challenge

Jolly
Graceful
Brave
Strong
Noble

Secret password is: **LOYAL**

6. Elara the Owl's Mystical Word Web

Adventure: Explore, Rescue
Journey, Discover, Voyage

Happy: Grateful, Cheerful, Enthusiastic, Joyful, Gleeful

Answers Page

7. Connie's Adventures

Here are the definitions of the words - did you use them correctly in your story?

Magical: Something that seems to use special powers, like in fairy tales or fantasy stories.

Mysterious: Something that is not known or understood and makes you curious to find out more.

Treasure: A collection of valuable things like gold, jewels, or rare items, often hidden and sought after in adventures.

Dazzle: To shine very brightly and impressively or to amaze someone with something wonderful.

Blossom: Flowers on a tree or plant, especially when they look beautiful and are seen in large numbers.

Playful: Full of fun and liking to play, often in a lighthearted or creative way.

Curious: Wanting to know about things, especially by asking questions and exploring.

Flutter: To move lightly and quickly, often used to describe how birds or butterflies move their wings.

8. The Code Breaker

Only a daring adventurer can uncover the unique knowledge hidden in the castle walls

9. The Unfinished Story

In the ***peaceful*** kingdom of Fireola, a brave knight named Sir Marcus embarked on a quest to find the ***fearsome*** dragon that had been ***frightening*** the villagers. Armed with his ***sharp*** sword and ***protective*** shield, he trekked through the ***dense*** forest. After days of searching, he finally found the dragon's ***lair*** in a mountain cave. To his surprise, the dragon was not fierce but rather ***friendly***. They talked for hours and realised that a misunderstanding had caused the ***conflict*** between the dragon and the village. Sir Marcus returned to the village, not with a story of battle but with a ***tale*** of friendship and peace.

Answers Page

10. The Second Door Challenge

Explore
Playful
Rescue
Magical
Happy

Secret password is: LAUGH

11. The Monarch's Menu

Here are the definitions of the words - did you use them correctly in the menu?

Brilliant: Very bright or smart.
Sumptuous: Very luxurious or rich.
Hearty: Strong and healthy, often used to describe a big, satisfying meal.
Wholesome: Good for your health.
Succulent: Juicy and tasty, especially used for food.
Rustic: Simple and often related to the countryside.
Fragrant: Having a pleasant and sweet smell.
Warm: Slightly hot or having a nice heat.
Surprise: Something unexpected or a sudden, unexpected event.
Fantastic: Really good or amazing.
Aromatic: Smelling very pleasant and strong.
Sizzling: Making a hissing sound like something cooking on a hot surface.

12. Pixie Pippin's Menu Muddle

Enormous: Very large; used to describe the huge size of a banquet feast
Delight: Great pleasure; the feeling guests have when enjoying delicious banquet dishes
Nourish: To provide banquet guests with the food necessary for growth and health
Abundant: Plentiful; used to describe a banquet table filled with lots of different foods
Skilful: Describes the talent of chefs in preparing and impressively presenting banquet meals
Mischief: Naughty or playful behaviour at a banquet, causing a little trouble
Quirky: Odd in a fun and interesting way, like an unusual banquet dish
Opulent: A very fancy banquet filled with expensive things

Answers Page

13. The Banquet Hall's Word Feast

Commence / Begin
Unseen / Hidden
Noble / Royal
Make-believe / Imaginary
Brave / Fearless

14. The Third Door Challenge

Mischief
Sizzling
Quirky
Opulent
Hearty

Secret password is: LUCKY

15. The Reflective Words

Fantastic
Yearn
Imitate
Clumsy
Surprise
Gentle
Harmony
Invisible

16. Mirror Word Magic

Melancholy and **Joyful** are opposites
Amiable and **Friendly** are the same
Courageous and **Fearless** are the same
Generous and **Mean** are opposites
Tranquil and **Serene** are the same
Curious and **Unconcerned** are opposite

17. The Hall of Mirrors Word Wonders

Accommodate: To make room or adjust to fit
Curiosity: A desire to learn or know about anything
Frequent: Happening or occurring often
Mischievous: Playfully naughty or troublesome
Opportunity: A chance for progress or advancement
Sincere: Free from pretence or deceit; genuine

18. The Fourth Door Challenge

Silent > **Huge** > **Observe** > **Strong** > **Lively**

The secret word is LIVELY

Answers Page

19. The Whispering Willow's Word Branches

Here are some ideas for words you could use:

Unhappy
Happiness
Happily
Playful
Replay
Overplay
Friendly
Unkind
Kindness
Kindly
Powerful
Overpower
Regrow
Overgrow

20. The Echoes of Ancient Stories

Show your work to a grown-up.
Are you proud of your short story?

21. The Raindrop Misspell Mystery

Scrol should be **scroll**
Echos should be **Echoes**
Seecret should be **secret**
Gobblin should be **goblin (twice)**
Eagar should be **eager**
Majic should be **magic (twice)**

22. The Fifth Door Challenge

At night, the **thunderstorm** rages overhead. A single **raindrop** falls and glistens in the **moonlight.**

23. Wizard Ivor's Enchanted Brew Formula

There is no right or wrong answer to this challenge. But did you have fun creating the names?

24. Wizard Ivor's Cauldron Conundrums

b - **whispering**
a - **emerald**
d - **stormy**
b - **maple**
a - **magical**
b - **twinkling**

Answers Page

25. The Sixth Door Challenge

1 down: Hard
2 across: Bark
3 across: Modern
4 down: Owl
5 across: Castle.

The secret password is SWORD

26. Wisteria's Enchanted Enigmas

Uncover
Courage
Antique
Mumble
Friend

27. The Tales of Tiles

In long-forgotten history, a strange tale is told of twelve brave soldiers, stood in a circle, who vanished in a flash of lightning.

28. The Seventh Door Challenge

The key is hidden beneath the ancient stone

29. The Chamber's Misplaced Mysteries

The castle had a round turret
Brave knights defended the kingdom from invaders
The forest was full of mysterious magic
The wizard used spells to protect the kingdom
The king hosted a feast in the castle hall

30. Jewels of Language

Weak/Feeble
Odd/Peculiar
Play/Frolic
Smell/Odour
Tall/Lofty
Ponder/Think
Destiny/Fate
Mistake/Blunder

31. The Vocabulary Vault

Integrity: Always telling the truth and being good, like a true and honest knight.
Majestic: Something really regal and grand, like this big, amazing castle.
Protagonist: The main person in a story, like Alfie, in his castle adventure.
Endeavour: Trying very hard to do something, like Alfie working hard to solve puzzles.
Illuminate: Making things bright or easy to understand, like lighting up a dark room or figuring out something hard.
Companion: A friend who joins you on adventures like the ones Alfie made in the castle.
Formidable: Something very strong and impressive, like a big, brave dragon.
Oath: A very important promise, like the ones knights make, to be brave.
Lavish: Very fancy and rich, like a big feast in the castle.
Exquisite: Very beautiful and special, like the wonderful treasures Alfie found.

The secret password is.....**magic spell**